THE Shakespeare Houses

Contents

Introduction: the five buildings 2
Shakespeare's Birthplace 6
Nash's House and New Place 12
Hall's Croft 16
Anne Hathaway's Cottage 20
Mary Arden's House 26
Further information ....inside back cover
Map of Stratford-upon-Avon ....outside back cover

Described by Roger Pringle
Director of the Shakespeare Birthplace Trust

Jarrold Publishing, Norwich
in association with the Shakespeare Birthplace Trust
Stratford-upon-Avon

Introduction: the five buildings

Portrait of Shakespeare by Gerard Soest (d. 1681)

A Family Saying Grace before a Meal (c. 1585) by Anthonius Claeissins, displayed at Hall's Croft

The Shakespeare Houses comprise five historic buildings situated in or near Stratford-upon-Avon that are directly associated with William Shakespeare and his family. Three are in the town itself: Shakespeare's Birthplace, in Henley Street, where the dramatist was born, in 1564, and grew up; Nash's House/New Place, in Chapel Street, a house acquired by Thomas Nash, the husband of Shakespeare's granddaughter, which overlooks the site where Shakespeare's retirement home once stood; and Hall's Croft, a house in Old Town, near Holy Trinity

Church, in which the dramatist's son-in-law and eldest daughter are believed to have lived before moving to New Place.

The other two Shakespeare Houses are located in Stratford's outlying countryside: Anne Hathaway's Cottage, in the village of Shottery, the farmhouse where Shakespeare's wife lived before her marriage in 1582; and Mary Arden's House, the farmstead in the village of Wilmcote, which was probably the girlhood home of Shakespeare's mother before she married John Shakespeare in about 1557.

The Shakespearian interest of the houses

Visiting these houses helps to satisfy our curiosity about Shakespeare, explaining much about his family and background, and reminding us that although his career took him to London, his native town was of significance throughout his life. Stratford was the place where he was born, went to school, attended church, met his wife, first watched plays, saw his children grow up, invested in property, retired and died.

With their room displays and other exhibits the houses also have much to say about the times in which Shakespeare lived. The 16th- and 17th-century collections of furnishings on view help to bring us close to the lifestyles of Shakespeare's contemporaries. We can learn about their eating, sleeping and washing habits, about their leisure hours, and even about their beliefs, fears and aspirations. The houses reveal other social aspects of Shakespeare's time and later, such as architectural styles, garden practice, and the customs of a rural society with which he was intimately connected. An understanding of this background is often a helpful accompaniment to an appreciation of Shakespeare's plays.

Carpenter's numbers on timbers at Hall's Croft

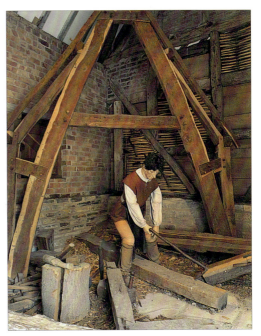

Exhibit showing a 16th-century carpenter at work, Glebe Farm (Mary Arden's House)

Architectural interest

The five buildings, although otherwise different in character, share a common architectural identity. Like many of the old houses in and around Stratford-upon-Avon, they were built from two principal materials, both derived from local sources. Each house is a timber-frame construction, using mainly oak, most of which was probably cut from woodland to the north of the town where pockets of the ancient Forest of Arden still stood. The other essential building material was stone, used for the foundation walls and chimneys, and for some of the floors. The stone for all five Shakespeare Houses was of a grey-blue variety of lias quarried at Wilmcote, the village three miles from Stratford, where Shakespeare's mother grew up.

The houses were prefabricated, that is to say the timber sections of the walls and roofs were prepared in advance on the ground, usually in a carpenter's yard, before being brought to the site, and then lifted into position and fitted together. On some of the beams, for example at the rear of Hall's Croft, the carpenter's numbering system can still be seen. This ensured that the different pieces could be easily identified and assembled on site. No glue, bolts or nails were used to join the timbers. Instead, the structure was held fast with joints cut in the timbers, usually the mortise and tenon kind, which were secured with wooden pegs. The oldest of the five houses is Anne Hathaway's Cottage, part of which dates from the mid-15th century and is constructed in a manner, prevalent in medieval times, which used long, curved timbers, or 'crucks', forming an upturned 'V' shape, to support the roof. The other Shakespeare Houses were built according to 16th-century practice, which had largely abandoned crucks in favour of a rectangular box-frame.

Once the frame of the building had been erected, the spaces between the timbers were filled with wattle and daub, consisting of small panels formed from interwoven sticks of hazel covered with a mixture of clay and straw, which was coated with lime plaster. Some of this infilling survives in the houses today, and at two of them, Shakespeare's Birthplace and Anne Hathaway's Cottage, an area of the surface plaster has been deliberately removed to expose the original wattle and daub.

Following the general custom in the 16th century, it is probable that the houses were painted over with a lime-wash, both inside and out. Some rooms have been treated in this traditional way to show visitors the original effect. The practice of creating a strong contrast between the timbers, sometimes painted black, and their adjoining panels coloured cream or white, was a fashion that did not become widespread until long after Shakespeare's time.

The houses were handmade by local carpenters and masons who were carrying on traditional

Cruck construction visible in Anne Hathaway's Cottage

skills, and it is a tribute to their workmanship and to the quality of their materials that so much survives of the original structures, despite inevitable later changes and restoration work. For centuries the buildings have coped with the weather and with the risk of timbers deteriorating through dampness or insect attack; in more recent times they have proved capable of absorbing large numbers of tourists. The houses, however, are not indestructible, and the Shakespeare Birthplace Trust is mindful of its responsibility to ensure they are carefully looked after, as well as to share and interpret this unique heritage for the enjoyment of visitors.

Lime-washed room in Anne Hathaway's Cottage

A tradition of sightseeing

Those who visit the Shakespeare Houses today are continuing a long tradition. Shakespeare's Birthplace and Anne Hathaway's Cottage were two of the first buildings of their kind to become tourist attractions, drawing secular pilgrims to their doors in the 18th century, at a time when Shakespeare was being acclaimed

as the national bard. That they and the other Shakespeare family houses survived was partly due to the early recognition of his fame and a deliberate effort to safeguard them, a process reflected in the purchase of his Birthplace as a national memorial in 1847, which brought the Shakespeare Birthplace Trust into existence. All five houses are now in the ownership and care of the Trust, and the income from visitors not only ensures the preservation of the buildings but allows the Trust to undertake wide-ranging educational programmes and conservation work.

The survival of the Shakespeare Houses, as aids to our understanding of the dramatist's life and times, is cause for celebration. No other famous writers, painters or musicians of his period, in any country, can be remembered and approached, outside their art, through the tangible presence today of several buildings with which they or their families were connected. The existence of the five houses, together with the wider heritage of Stratford, which includes his school and the church where he worshipped and is buried, partly compensates for the relatively few documents of personal interest about Shakespeare that have been preserved. The houses help to provide a context in which to consider the man who, 400 years ago, wrote plays that have captured the hearts and minds of readers and audiences throughout the world.

Above: The Birthplace with early photographers

Left: The auction of the Birthplace, 16 September 1847

Right: Anne Hathaway's Cottage

Shakespeare's Birthplace

William Shakespeare not only grew up in this building but was associated with it all his life. It is quite likely that he and his wife lived there for some time after their marriage in 1582. He certainly inherited the house when his father died in 1601 and bequeathed it on his own death in 1616 to his eldest daughter. The Birthplace is in fact one of the very few surviving objects that unquestionably belonged to him.

Several documents exist to show that John Shakespeare, the dramatist's father, acquired the property on this site in two separate transactions, the main part being purchased in 1556, probably shortly after it had been built. In his son's day the family home was a fairly spacious property, reflecting John Shakespeare's relative affluence; besides his craft as a glovemaker, he was for some years a dealer in wool on a considerable scale and was also involved in money-lending. Over a long period he was a prominent member of Stratford's town council, serving as bailiff (mayor) in 1568.

The Visitors' Centre exhibition

Visitors begin their tour at the Visitors' Centre, where an exhibition tells the story of

Shakespeare's life and background. The exhibition features many original items, including a desk in use at the Stratford grammar school in Shakespeare's time and a first edition of Shakespeare's collected plays, as well as specially constructed scenes and a scale model of the Globe theatre.

The displays in the Birthplace

The displays in the furnished rooms are based closely on evidence relating to the houses of craftsmen and merchants in 16th-century Stratford and elsewhere. Where possible, original furnishings are shown but some authentically made replica items have been introduced to give a fully detailed picture of the kind of family home in which William Shakespeare grew up. Modern techniques reproduce the lighting conditions of a pre-electric age and, as was the custom in the past, most walls, including the timbers, have been limewashed.

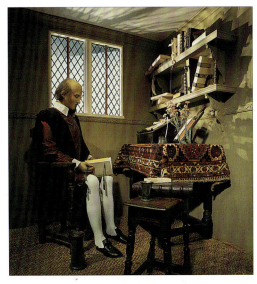

Opposite: *The front of the Birthplace*

Above: *Shakespeare's study, a reconstruction in the Visitors' Centre exhibition*

Below: *The parlour*

A tour of the house

Visitors enter the building through a small room that was once part of a separate house, occupied in the first part of the 17th century by Shakespeare's sister Joan Hart and her family. The displays provide an introduction to the Birthplace.

The parlour

A doorway leads to the first room of the Birthplace itself, the parlour.

Such rooms were used for general daytime domestic purposes, and often doubled up as bedchambers. The plain, textile-hung bed, copied from a rare 16th-century example at Anne Hathaway's Cottage, has homespun blankets and curtains of a weave and colour common in Shakespeare's time. The ancient floor of broken slabs of stone may be original.

The spinning-wheel and winder are reminders that wool-processing was a regular activity, particularly in a household like the Shakespeares', where John was a wool-dealer. Bright, painted cloths frequently decorated the walls of ordinary 16th-century houses. The cloth here has a design copied from a mural painting, in Oxford, dated *c.* 1570.

The hall

This room was where the family gathered for meals in Shakespeare's time. The large, original fireplace has a spit for roasting and other cooking-utensils. The table is set as it would have been in the 16th century. Period furniture includes a stool and bench, both in gothic style, and a cupboard displaying pewter tableware. One wall-hanging copies the design on part of an original painted cloth, now in the Victoria and Albert Museum, and another features the biblical story of the Prodigal Son, copied from a tapestry of the period. Beyond the hall is the cross-passage, with the doorway on the right being the original entrance to the house from the street.

The glover's workshop

On the far side of the cross-passage is the room thought to have been John Shakespeare's workshop. Examples of the 'dressed' animal skins used by 16th-century glovemakers are displayed, together with tools for preparing leather and cutting and sewing gloves. It is also likely this room was John's shop from where gloves and other leather wares, such as purses, were sold. Evidence for the influence of his father's craft can be found in those plays of Shakespeare that contain knowledgeable references to leather preparation and glove-making.

The upstairs rooms

At the top of the stairs are two rooms. The first is furnished with a half-headed bed and replica painted cloths of 'antique work' whose design

Above left: *The hall of the Birthplace*

Above right: *16th-century woodcut of a glover's workshop*

Right: *The glover's workshop*

is copied from a wall-painting. The second room, originally another bedchamber, now contains displays about the history of the house, including its story as a place of Shakespearian pilgrimage. Amongst the exhibits is a window on which 19th-century visitors to the house scratched their names, including Sir Walter Scott and Thomas Carlyle.

'Shakespeare's birthroom'

Another bedchamber is entered next which, according to a tradition established by the mid-18th century, was the room in which Shakespeare was born. The textiles, which accurately follow 16th-century examples, include the red and green woollen bed curtains and the painted wall-cloths with floral motifs. Stored under the main bed is a replica, wheeled 'truckle bed', used by children or servants. The cradle, washing-tub, baby clothes and toys are exact copies of originals dating from Shakespeare's time.

The rear wing

Before entering two small rooms that were also bedchambers, the original, narrow staircase can be seen. The rear room has a display documenting the ownership of the house by Shakespeare's family and descendants. This back wing was probably added to the main building shortly after the death of Shakespeare's father in 1601, when part of the house became an inn.

The kitchen and buttery

Modern stairs lead to a room long used as a kitchen, which dates from the early 17th century, when the rear wing was built. Before then, when Shakespeare was growing up in the house, there was almost certainly a detached kitchen at the back.

Above: 'Shakespeare's birthroom'
Below: The kitchen

The displays now focus on the preparation of meals and include kitchen items of Shakespeare's time and a table, with a trestle base, showing centuries of use. The open hearth features an iron fire basket for coal, of a kind mentioned as being in the kitchen in 1627. The adjoining buttery has original and replica ceramics, mainly used for the storage of food.

The garden

The present layout of the garden derives largely from the mid-19th century, and features many plants mentioned by Shakespeare. In his time the garden would have been cultivated mainly for useful household produce. This is reflected today in an emphasis given to herbs, fruit trees and fruit bushes that were common in the 16th century. The herbaceous borders, best viewed from the end of the central path, and the beds of old-fashioned roses recall the delight in flowers expressed by Shakespeare and many of his contemporaries.

Above: *The garden of the Birthplace*

Below: *The procession of Garrick's Shakespeare festival outside the Birthplace in 1769*

Later history

From the time of Shakespeare's death until the early 19th century the house retained a connection with his family. His sister Joan lived in part of the building until her death in 1646, and it was subsequently owned or occupied by her descendants until 1806. In 1847 the house was sold at auction and passed to the Shakespeare Birthplace Trust for preservation as a national memorial.

The Birthplace as a visitor attraction

For 250 years the Birthplace has been a place of homage for admirers of Shakespeare. It was attracting visitors by the mid-18th century and became a focus of attention during the first Shakespeare festival, held in the town in 1769 and organised by the famous actor David Garrick. Improved communications by road and, later, rail, together with the growth of Shakespeare's worldwide fame, brought increasing international patronage.

Amongst the 19th-century visitors who came to the Birthplace were many well-known writers, including John Keats (1817), Maria Edgeworth (1819), Sir Walter Scott (1821),

Thomas Carlyle (1824), Charles Dickens (1838), Alfred Tennyson (1840), Harriet Beecher Stowe (1854), Herman Melville (1857), Henry Longfellow (1868), Mark Twain (1873) and Thomas Hardy (1896).

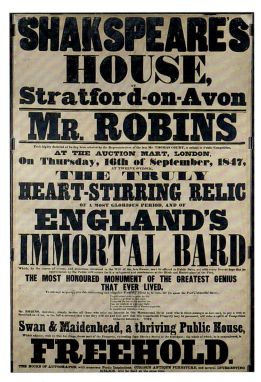

Above: Poster advertising the sale of 1847
Above left: Charles Dickens' signature in the Visitors' Book
Below: Drawing of the Birthplace in 1807, by Henry Edridge, when it was still part of a continuous row of buildings fronting the street

Nash's House & New Place

Nash's House adjoins the site of New Place, Shakespeare's Stratford home for the last eighteen years of his life, which was pulled down in the 18th century. The two buildings were closely associated through being owned by relations of Shakespeare's family. Nash's House belonged to Thomas Nash, a wealthy Stratford property-owner, who married Shakespeare's granddaughter Elizabeth Hall in 1626, ten years after the dramatist's death. At this time New Place was occupied by Elizabeth's parents, Shakespeare's daughter, Susanna, and her husband, John Hall.

Thomas Nash does not seem to have lived in Nash's House, but following his marriage to Elizabeth the couple appear to have resided at New Place with the Halls. When Thomas Nash died in 1647 he left Nash's House to his wife, and it remained her property until she died in 1670. Elizabeth, Shakespeare's last direct descendant, continued to live for a while next door at New Place after a second marriage, to John Barnard in 1649, before moving away to his family home in Northamptonshire.

Nash's House and New Place were linked not only through ownership and physical proximity. At different times in the past what is now the Great Garden of New Place has belonged to Nash's House, and some of the latter's garden became part of the New Place estate. Given their interrelated history, it is appropriate that today the site of New Place is accessed through Nash's House.

A tour of Nash's House

Nash's House, on its ground floor, gives a good idea of the kind of furnishings that would have filled the rooms of New Place next door when the Shakespeares, Halls and Nashs lived there during the reigns of James I and Charles I.

Left: New Place and Nash's House as they may have looked in 1597 (drawing by Pat Hughes) and Nash's House today

Right: The entrance hall of Nash's House

Below left: The 'cupboard of boxes'

Below right: The parlour

Entrance hall

The hall has notable chests and cupboards, some with fine carving and inlay work, but a piece that attracts special attention is the plainest, a 'cupboard of boxes'. Commissioned in 1594 by the Stratford town council, to whom it still belongs, the cupboard took sixteen and a half days to make, cost over £3 and was used to store documents. The portrait of Joyce Clopton (1562–1637) is by a follower of Marcus Gheeraerts: one of her ancestors, Hugh Clopton, built New Place a century before Shakespeare owned it, and later members of the family owned New Place and Nash's House. Beside the fireplace is a mid-17th-century lantern clock.

Parlour and kitchen

The parlour was originally two rooms (hence a fireplace at each end), and now provides another setting for furniture reflecting the style and taste of affluent town households in the first half of the 17th century. The ornately carved dining-table, with bulbous legs, and the court cupboard, used for displaying plates, with its inlaid frieze of leaf and flower pattern, have particular appeal.

The paintings include a 16th-century oil, believed to be Flemish and to depict the story of Susanna and the Elders, which shows garden features of the period. Also displayed on the walls are two tapestry panels, dated about 1600, which were woven in the famous Sheldon workshop at Barcheston, ten miles from Stratford.

Left: *One of the two Sheldon tapestry panels*

Right: *Portrait of David Garrick (1717–79)*

Below: *Saxon brooch from the archaeological collection*

Beyond the parlour, in a later extension to the house, is a small kitchen displayed as it might have been in the 19th century.

The upstairs rooms

Unlike the other Shakespeare Houses, the upper floor is not furnished in a domestic manner but, instead, accommodates museum displays, mostly illustrating aspects of Stratford's long and varied history. The first room, off the top of the stairs, contains archaeological finds connected with the town's prehistoric origins and its subsequent Roman and Anglo-Saxon settlements.

In one of the rooms facing the street, there are exhibits relating to Stratford in the medieval period and during Shakespeare's time, and to the history of New Place. A further room includes items linked with the town's first Shakespeare festival, arranged by the distinguished actor David Garrick in 1769.

The site of New Place

A passageway beyond the entrance hall leads to the site and gardens of New Place. Shakespeare purchased the house, probably from his London theatre earnings, in 1597, when he was thirty-three, and eventually retired to it and died under its roof. Described in about 1540 as a 'pretty house of brick and timber', it was also one of the largest residences in the town. The principal part, where Shakespeare lived, was set back from the road and accessed by way of an outer range of buildings that faced onto Chapel Street and Chapel Lane, enclosing a courtyard in front of the main house.

New Place was pulled down, or at least substantially rebuilt, around 1702, and the new house erected in its place was itself demolished in 1759. The only parts of the original structure to survive are small portions of foundation walls, some brickwork and a couple of wells. Fragmentary though these remains are, the site has a special significance because Shakespeare owned it for over a third of his life. Immediately to the south is the Guild Chapel, the appearance of which is essentially unchanged since Shakespeare looked in that direction from his house and garden.

The Knot Garden

When Shakespeare bought New Place it stood in extensive grounds: his property deeds mention two gardens and two orchards. The whole of his original estate is now preserved as garden space.

Close to where Shakespeare's main apartments were located is an Elizabethan-style

Right: The site of New Place, backed by Nash's House

Below: The Knot Garden, looking towards the Guild Chapel

knot garden created in 1919–20, and approached through a palisade. The four beds or 'knots' incorporate an interweaving design created from dwarf herbs or shrubs, which is closely based on illustrations in the garden books of Shakespeare's time. Flowers fill the spaces between the outline pattern. Many of the plants used are mentioned by Shakespeare, although some later species have been introduced to help create the colourful effects sought by Elizabethan gardeners.

The Great Garden

A trellis-work tunnel or pergola leads from the Knot Garden to a terrace overlooking the Great Garden, which can also be reached from Chapel Lane.

With its box and yew hedges, expanse of lawn (boasting an old mulberry said to have been grown from a cutting taken from a tree planted by Shakespeare) and its flower beds and borders, the garden is an attractive haven close to the centre of Stratford. Shakespeare must also have valued the beauty and quiet of his own garden, situated in this very place, especially when he retreated to New Place to escape the pressures of his theatre career in the capital.

Hall's Croft

Much is known about John Hall, a physician who married Shakespeare's eldest daughter, Susanna. In particular, as some of the displays at Hall's Croft show, the information that we have about his medical practice in Stratford makes him one of the best-documented provincial doctors of early modern England.

Hall, who took a degree at Cambridge and probably pursued his medical studies abroad, appears to have come to Stratford a year or two before his marriage in 1607. Soon after Shakespeare died in 1616, the Halls moved to New Place, the dramatist's impressive house in Chapel Street. The evidence regarding where they lived before going to New Place is not conclusive. However, in 1811 a local historian referred to a document indicating that the doctor lived in Old Town, and by around the mid-19th century the house now called Hall's Croft was being identified in print and in illustration as the home of John and Susanna Hall. It is now known that the main part of this fine timbered building was put up in 1613. Given the traditions and the absence of any evidence to the contrary, it is reasonable to infer that the house, one of only a handful of buildings that stood in the street in Shakespeare's time, was erected for the Halls and served as their home for a few years, before Shakespeare's death led them to move to New Place.

The house

For most of its history, Hall's Croft has been the home of relatively prosperous, often professional people, although for about twenty-five years in the mid-19th century it also served as a small school. In 1949 the building was bought by the Shakespeare Birthplace Trust and, after alterations and repairs, opened to the public two years later.

When first erected the house was simpler than it now appears, consisting of a small range

Top: *Hall's Croft in the early 17th century, a conjectural drawing by Pat Hughes*

Above: *The front exterior of Hall's Croft today*

Left: The parlour

Right: Child's high chair, early 17th century

Below: Painting of a patient and doctor, c. 1660

facing the street, with a separate building towards the rear. Subsequent changes, some possibly undertaken by Dr Hall, extended the original house and integrated it with the building at the back.

A tour of the house

The room displays are intended to reflect John Hall's comparative wealth and his status as the leading physician in the local community, with most of the furniture dating from the first half of the 17th century.

The entrance hall and parlour

The spacious hall, with its stone fireplace and panel-back armchairs, dating from about 1640, signals a house of some presence. Leading off the hall is the parlour, the principal room of the house. In the centre of the room is a draw-leaf table of the kind that was fashionable in the first half of the 17th century. On either side of the fireplace are the two most ornate chairs in the Shakespeare Birthplace Trust's collections: a child's high chair made of ash and an armchair of yew, both outstanding examples of turned furniture of this period.

The large oil-painting on panel, depicting a family saying grace before a meal (see page 2), is by Anthonius Claeissins (c. 1538–1613). Painted in Bruges in about 1585, it features a pious merchant or professional family whose dress, jewellery, tableware and furniture were similar to those seen in the prosperous households of Shakespeare's Stratford. Above the fireplace, the painting of a wooded landscape with a hunt is by Salomon Rombouts (c. 1645–1702).

The passageway

At the end of the parlour, steps lead to a passageway with small windows looking onto the garden. Items of interest here include a mid-17th-century bookbinding press and a copy of a portrait of the poet Michael Drayton, a Warwickshire contemporary of Shakespeare, whom Dr Hall treated for a fever.

The consulting-room

The passage leads to a small room furnished in the manner of a consulting-room of John Hall's time. Two small, 17th-century Dutch paintings show respectively a patient consulting a doctor and an apothecary at work.

Above: Mural cupboard

Right: The kitchen

Below centre: Portrait of a mother and child, 1627

The cupboard table is a rare piece dating from about 1520, and on the side wall is an early 17th-century oak and fruitwood cupboard with fine parquetry work. The items displayed on the table include a pestle and mortar for pounding medicines and some English delft jars, made in London around 1600, which were used for storing medicine and ointments. The colourful drug jars on the shelf are Italian and of the kind that were imported into England during the 17th century.

Back hall

Steps down from the consulting-room lead to a back hall where there is an attractive 17th-century mural cupboard and a seat-table with a hinged top, allowing it to be used for either purpose, with a storage compartment below.

The kitchen

The kitchen has a massive fireplace equipped with cooking-utensils and an 18th-century wrought-iron spit assembly, complete with drip pan and accessories. The furniture dates from the 17th century.

Staircase and landing

Opposite the foot of the stairs is a fine painting of a mother and child, dated 1627 and attributed to the Amsterdam portraitist Nicolaes Eliasz. The elegant staircase is mid-17th century. To the left of the landing is a painting, *Death and the Maiden*, English School, *c.* 1570, which is a rare example of an allegorical picture on the theme of mortality surviving from the period.

17th-century Italian drug jars

The principal bedroom

This room, with its barrel-vaulted ceiling, features an oak tester bed with delicately carved, 16th-century posts. The mid-17th-century clothes-press, probably of Dutch origin, has finely carved features, including lion masks. The ornate chest dates from about 1630, and the cupboard pierced with ventilation panels is a few years later. Near the bed a 17th-century stool with a hinged lid is a reminder of the sanitary arrangements of the period. The portrait is of Mary Harvey, painted in 1620 when she was aged twenty-four. The picture's inscription also records that she died two years later. She was related to the family of William Harvey, the famous physician, to whom John Hall refers in his medical notebook.

Exhibition room

A door from the bedchamber leads to a galleried room, which was once divided into bedrooms. It now contains an exhibition illustrating John Hall's life and aspects of medicine in his time. His reputation as a doctor spread well beyond Stratford, and after his death some of his medical notes were published, in 1657, under the title *Select Observations on English Bodies*. The book, a copy of which is displayed, describes the many illnesses that Hall encountered and the treatments he administered.

Top: The principal bedroom

Centre: The title page of Select Observations on English Bodies

Right: The garden

Servant's bedchamber

A doorway from the exhibition room leads to a bedroom furnished as a servant's room, with a simple 17th-century bed and stool. A passageway goes back to the landing by way of a small chamber that gives good views across the garden.

The garden

A door from the back hall opens into a walled garden. A long path, with a herbaceous border on each side, leads to a sundial and arbour with a fine view of the house. The old tree on the lawn is a mulberry, and close by is a formal bed containing many of the herbs mentioned by John Hall in his medical notebook. Like all physicians of his time, Hall's remedies consisted mainly of elaborate herbal preparations.

Shakespeare's considerable medical knowledge almost certainly derived in part from his friendship with John Hall, who was doubtless the dramatist's own physician and attended him on his deathbed in 1616. When Hall himself died in 1635, the Stratford church register referred to him as '*medicus peritissimus*' (a most skilled doctor). He left possessions and money worth over £1,000 to be divided equally between his wife, Susanna, and his daughter, Elizabeth, and gave his 'study of books' to his son-in-law, Thomas Nash.

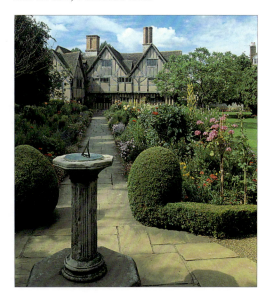

Anne Hathaway's Cottage

Situated in the village of Shottery, a mile from Stratford, Anne Hathaway's Cottage was the home of William Shakespeare's wife before they married in 1582, when she was twenty-six and he was eighteen. Her father, Richard Hathaway, was a farmer, and the family home was known as Hewlands. The house remained a working farm until the 19th century, and was lived in by Hathaways and descendants of the family for 300 years.

The building was attracting occasional visitors in the second half of the 18th century and by the 1820s had assumed the name Anne Hathaway's Cottage. Prominent Victorian writers who visited the house included Alfred Tennyson, in 1840, and Charles Dickens, in 1852. The property was purchased in 1892 by the Shakespeare Birthplace Trust for permanent preservation; fifty years earlier there had been talk that its owner was intending to demolish the house in favour of a modern building.

The view from the garden

Besides its romantic associations, as the place where the teenage Shakespeare courted his future wife, the Hathaway home has also come to be regarded as a quintessential country cottage. The view of the house from across its garden has inspired countless paintings and photographs, and represents one of the most familiar images of 'old England'. Built from timber, stone and brick, with a thatched roof that partly conceals its diamond-paned dormer windows, the house now rests in a pretty setting. However, the garden only began to assume its present form in the latter part of the 19th century. The area in front of the house largely consisted of a farmyard until the middle of that century, at which point it started to be more formally cultivated, mainly with vegetables at first, and then more decoratively with a wide variety of traditional country flowers planted in the somewhat crowded manner that is characteristic of the typical Victorian cottage garden.

The house

The Hathaway farmhouse was built in two main stages. Much of the lower portion, as seen on the right from the garden and consisting of about two-thirds of the present building, dates from the mid-15th century and probably comprised the extent of the house in which Anne Hathaway grew up. The taller portion was added in the 17th century, possibly by Bartholomew Hathaway, Anne's eldest brother, who died in 1624. Some refurbishment occurred in the late 17th century: the central chimney was rebuilt in 1697 and bears the initials of a John Hathaway.

The furnishings

When the Shakespeare Birthplace Trust bought the Cottage in 1892 it also acquired some items of furniture that had been used in

Above: *Shakespeare's marriage licence bond, 28 November 1582*

Right: *The hall, with the late 17th-century dresser*

The buttery and 16th-century earthenware watering-pot

the house by members of the Hathaway family and their descendants. Since then additions have been made to the room displays but the Trust's policy is to show the building much as it was at the time of its purchase. Visitors, therefore, see furniture ranging in date from the 16th to the 19th century.

A tour of the house

The farmhouse is entered by way of a cross-passage, on the left of which is the hall or principal living-room.

The hall

On one side of the hall's wide, open hearth is a bacon cupboard, inserted in 1697. An old tradition claims that the elm-boarded settle near the fireplace was sat on by William and Anne when they were courting, but it has to be said that the piece dates mainly from a later period. However, the settle, together with the late 17th-century dresser displaying tableware used at different periods in the house, and the early 18th-century table are all family pieces that have been in the room for generations.

Buttery and cold room

A stone-flagged passage leads from the hall past two small rooms, situated on the cooler side of the house: the buttery and the cold room. A list of Bartholomew Hathaway's goods, made in 1624, mentions two barrels and a powdering-tub (for salting meat) in the buttery. Used for storing ale and general provisions, the buttery may also have served as a dairy and now contains a collection of butter- and cheese-making implements.

Displayed in the cold room, which has traditional lime-washed walls, are various items for the house and garden, ranging from a 16th-century earthenware watering-pot to a 19th-century wash-tub.

The upstairs rooms

Running the length of the house upstairs is a series of rooms used as sleeping-quarters or for storage space. The chamber on the left at the top of the stairs has a 17th-century half-headed bed and a chair made of straw, which is a rare piece dating perhaps from a similar period.

The next room contains the best-known family heirloom: a finely carved, oak tester

Right: The oak tester bed

Below: A rare early straw chair

Below right: The kitchen

bed, which may well have been the one valued at £3 in 1624, on the death of Anne Hathaway's brother.

Another four-poster bed dating from Anne's time, with hangings of homespun cloth, is in the next chamber. Plain beds of this kind and date are now very uncommon.

A doorway leads to a small storeroom. At this point a pair of curved beams, known as 'crucks', pegged together at the top, can be seen. The timbers used in this part of the house have been scientifically dated to 1462–3. Some of the wattle-and-daub panels, made from interwoven twigs plastered with clay and lime-washed over, have been deliberately exposed to view.

The kitchen

A staircase leads down to a spacious, stone-flagged kitchen dominated by an open fireplace. To the left of the hearth is a bread oven, with its wooden 'stop', or door, and equipment used in baking.

The museum room

Turning into the cross-passage, visitors emerge at the rear of the house before re-entering it through a parlour. Displayed in this room are items associated with the Cottage and its occupants, including a 17th-century bed-sheet and bolster belonging to the Hathaway family, and paintings of the house from different periods.

The orchard

Returning to the garden, a path to the right passes a vegetable patch where old varieties of beans, peas, cabbages, etc. are grown. Ahead is the orchard, planted with traditional varieties of apples and pears, and providing a view across fields once worked by the Hathaways and neighbouring farmers.

Above: Detail of the embroidery on the 17th-century bed-sheet

Right: A view of the house from the orchard

Below: Mrs Mary Baker, who lived in Anne Hathaway's Cottage for much of the 19th century and acted as a guide

Below right: The vegetable garden

The Shakespeare Tree Garden

To the right of the exit from the main site is the Shakespeare Tree Garden, created in 1988 and planted with most of the trees mentioned in Shakespeare's plays.

Walks

Opposite the Cottage, on the other side of the road, are two pretty walks that offer views of Shottery Brook and its environs. It has been suggested that the description of Ophelia's drowning in *Hamlet* and some of the woodland scenes in *As You Like It* were partly inspired by Shakespeare's recollection of the countryside around his wife's home. Something of that rural world which Shakespeare knew and described vividly can still be sensed in Shottery today.

Top: Shottery Brook
Left and below: Shottery Brook walk and pond

Mary Arden's House

Above: *The exterior of Mary Arden's House*
Below: *Elizabethan woodcut depicting harvesting*

This farmhouse, situated in the village of Wilmcote, takes its name from Shakespeare's mother. She was the daughter of Robert Arden, a farmer of means, whose main landholding was in Wilmcote. Robert died in 1556 and luckily his will and inventory have survived, giving details about his family and the contents of his house and barns.

Robert Arden left his Wilmcote property, then called Asbies, to Mary, the youngest of eight daughters. His bequest was probably made shortly in advance of her marriage to

Right: A rear view of Mary Arden's House

Below: One of two Romany caravans

John Shakespeare. The documentary evidence is insufficient to prove the whereabouts of the Arden home in Wilmcote for certain, but the identification of it as the building now known as Mary Arden's House relies on a long tradition that goes back to the 18th century. It was in this spirit that the Shakespeare Birthplace Trust purchased the 16th-century farmhouse in 1930 and carried out repairs to ensure its survival. Later, in 1968, the Trust acquired and later restored the nearby Glebe Farm, which now forms part of the overall site seen by visitors.

To visit Mary Arden's House and its centuries-old stone outbuildings, still surrounded by the fields of the village where Shakespeare's grandfather farmed and his mother spent her girlhood, is a valuable experience for anyone who wishes to understand the dramatist's family origins and the rural environment from which he came. The depictions of country scenes and rustic characters in his plays probably owe much to his experience of the landscape and farming communities around Stratford. He describes memorably many of the sights and sounds of the countryside: wild flowers, birds and animals; farmers at work in the fields; changes of weather and season; sports and folk customs.

When Mary Arden was growing up in Wilmcote, the village was on the edge of the Forest of Arden, the ancient tract of woodland from which her family name derived. Much of Shakespeare's romantic comedy *As You Like It* is set in the Forest of Arden, and although the imagined wood is a more exotic place than any Warwickshire equivalent, the play's descriptive passages have a detailed, intimate quality that seems rooted in a personal knowledge of the dramatist's native countryside. Part of his rural world was the Arden property at Wilmcote, and it is worth noting that when a dispute about it arose in 1588 the twenty-four-year-old Shakespeare was mentioned in the relevant document, along with his father and mother. We can believe he knew the place well.

Left: The horse-powered cider-mill

Right: The dovecote with 650 nesting-holes

Below: The open-fronted byre

A tour of the site

Today, the visitor approaches Mary Arden's House through two farmyards.

The rickyard

The first farmyard, known as the rickyard, features twelve 'staddle' stones standing on the grassed area. When a wooden frame was placed across these stones, ricks of hay or straw could be built on them, away from the damp and from rodents. The open-fronted buildings around the yard are of relatively recent date and contain items from the Shakespeare Countryside Museum collections, more of which are displayed in most of the barns and other outbuildings on the site. Exhibits in the rickyard include local farm waggons, a horse-drawn fire-engine used in Stratford and the surrounding countryside during the 19th century, and two Romany caravans.

The old farmyard

A path leads under a stone archway (once used for sheltering hay or corn waggons) to a second farmyard, at the rear of Mary Arden's House. The buildings on the left comprise a small barn containing a horse-powered cider-mill, an open-fronted byre and a dovecote with over 650 nesting-holes. The original farmyard, extending over the area that is now grass, was for certain a busy working-space for generations of farmers. Apart from bees and poultry, Robert Arden's inventory of 1556 mentions the presence on his farm of various animals, including oxen, cows, sheep, horses and pigs. Water for the house came from wells, one of which was sited in the farmyard where the present pump now stands.

Mary Arden's House

Entrance to the house is from the back by way of a cross-passage that divides the kitchen, on the right, from the hall.

The kitchen

Most meals were prepared and cooked in the kitchen, using the large open fireplace. Robert Arden's goods included an assortment of pots, pans and other cooking-utensils of the kind displayed in the room. Meat was roasted on the spit, and the food was eaten out of bowls or off wooden platters or pewter plates.

Left: The hall

Below: The bread ark

Bottom: The bed-chamber with the iron-bound trunk

The hall

The hall was originally open to the roof before a first floor was inserted, perhaps at the end of the 16th century, to provide further bedroom space upstairs. The room's main features are its inglenook fireplace and the country furniture; the latter includes an early 16th-century aumbry cupboard with two carved portrait panels, and a 17th-century dining-table whose top is marked for playing the game of shove-halfpenny.

The dairy

Leading from the hall is the dairy, with its sunken floor, occupying a cool position at the back of the house. The butter- and cheese-making utensils are similar to those in use in Shakespeare's time. A 19th-century mousetrap hangs on the wall.

The parlour

Steps lead down to a wing of the house, comprising a ground-floor parlour and a bedroom upstairs, which was added to the original building, probably in the 17th century. This extension provided extra living- and sleeping-space for the family or their hired farm-workers. The parlour is furnished simply with a table, benches, a 16th-century chest with linen-fold carved panels, and a large 17th-century bread ark.

The upstairs rooms

The house has four chambers upstairs, which served originally as sleeping-quarters and storage areas. The furniture is mainly of the 17th century but the last bedchamber has an iron-bound, wooden trunk dating from about 1500.

The stable and the Great Barn

Across the farmyard at the back of Mary Arden's House is a stable. For centuries, before mechanisation came to the land, horses played a central role in all farming operations other than those performed by oxen or by manual labour. The list of Robert Arden's belongings, made in 1556, included four horses and three colts.

Next to the stable is the Great Barn, which now houses a further part of the Trust's Shakespeare Countryside Museum collections. The exhibits here illustrate some of the principal farming tasks undertaken in a pre-mechanised age, arranged according to the four seasons of the year. Although most of the tools date from the 18th and 19th centuries, many had not changed their basic forms since Shakespeare's time.

The pastimes enjoyed by country people are represented in the museum collections and also, in live fashion, by the falconry displays that take place throughout the year in the field beyond Mary Arden's House. Shakespeare frequently refers in his plays to the popular sport of falconry.

A path across the field adjoining Mary Arden's House leads to the Glebe Farm.

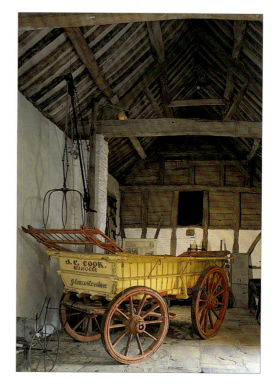

Above: *The Great Barn and stable*
Right: *A farm cart on display*

The largest outbuilding houses a working forge, and opposite it, on the other side of the Glebe farmyard, is a 19th-century pigsty and an old granary with a dog-kennel under its steps.

Although some of the farmhouse dates from Shakespeare's time, various additions and alterations were made later, with much of the building having been faced with brick, probably in the 18th century. The ground-floor rooms are now furnished as they might have looked in the early years of the 20th century.

The Glebe Farm

Until its restoration in 1986, the Glebe Farm was a separate property. The Shakespeare Countryside Museum is continued in the old outbuildings, with one barn containing displays about the local use of timber and stone for building purposes, and another showing exhibits relating to the crafts of the carpenter, cooper and wheelwright.

Kitchen, living-room and dairy

On entering the rear door of Glebe Farm, the back kitchen is on the right, showing a washday in progress.

Opposite is the living-room, where all the main activities of the house took place, including cooking. An early 20th-century iron

Above: Exterior of Glebe Farm

Above right: Working in the forge

Right: Washday in the scullery at Glebe Farm

Right: Glebe Farm's garden

Below: The 18th-century long-case clock in the parlour

Bottom right: Some of the farm animals

range fills the original fireplace, and the old bread oven can be seen in the cupboard on the far right. The plain table (at which an elderly lady sits plucking a hen), dresser, chairs and other furnishings evoke farmhouse life of 100 years ago.

The dairy, situated off the living-room, is well prepared for butter- and cheese-making. The equipment includes a large butter-worker in the right-hand corner and a box-churn on the stone slab in the left-hand corner.

The parlour and cold store

The parlour, situated beyond the living-room, was used mainly for special occasions, and contains examples of family heirlooms, such as the 18th-century clock and pieces of 19th-century china.

The cold store, vital for the keeping of food before the days of refrigerators, can be seen from the parlour, although its original door led in from the farmyard.

The Glebe Farm garden

On leaving the Glebe Farm, a narrow passageway on the left leads to the garden in front of the house, which is planted in a typical country fashion with fruit trees, vegetables, herbs and traditional flowers and shrubs. Here also is one of the two original wells that supplied the water for the farmhouse.

Wildlife, farm animals and the Field Walk

The site covers several acres and gives the visitor an opportunity to enjoy the countryside near the two farmhouses. At the end of the rickyard, behind the Great Barn, is a pond that provides a habitat for ducks and other wildlife. Close by, a circular walk begins its course around fields where some of the wild flowers described by Shakespeare can be seen in season, such as 'the pale primrose', 'blue-veined violets', 'the freckled cowslip, burnet and green clover' and 'rough thistles'.

The walk passes pens containing rare breeds of poultry, and the Trust's Cotswold sheep and Longhorn cows are often grazing in the fields. The fifty-two sheep recorded as belonging to Robert Arden in 1556 may well have been a Cotswold flock. Perhaps, like Corin the shepherd in *As You Like It*, Robert would have agreed that 'the greatest of my pride is to see my ewes graze and my lambs suck'.